AF477833

Time and the Word Machine

Edward Milton McWhorter

VANTAGE PRESS
New York

To Carlyn, who drew the pictures that gather and emblazon the many meanings of words in the text into singular purpose and to whom I am devoted

Contents

Part II: The Tree of the World

The Tree of the World Model

Part III: The Story of Stonehenge

Stonehenge Model

Introduction

There is not good and evil in the world, there is only goodness. Evil is only emptiness in the cup waiting to be filled with goodness. Goodness is the knightly quest of the golden chalice of mankind.

We must learn to think positively, not negatively on those points of greatest concern to our Spiritual development. There is not light or darkness, there is only light, the presence or the absence of electromagnetic radiation, there is not sound or silence, there is only the presence of energy vibrating in a medium of compressible form. There is not hot or cold, there is only the heat-generating principle of thermo molecular interaction. Think positively who you are in the Becoming time. There is not Life or death, there is only eternal Life and it is infinite.

This is the story of the Chaldean word-line and the word machine which the early Greeks and Egyptians called the Ennead. It is described as the Neters Spirit Catcher by the ancients of Heliopolis. The Sanskrit verse of the Aryan scriptures speak of this as a gridwork, as the expectant point covered by the form matrix which reach crosswise as an omnipresent nexus of meaning in gridlike form. Yet it must be noted that in each Asking, regardless of the belief, there is a knightly quest for the holy grail of truth. The knightly endeavor of all mankind.

This is also the story of the Tree of the World, the Tree

Knowers knowledge of ancient times, a story that is still very much alive and told today.

And finally, this is also the story of Stonehenge that languishes in indifferent interpretation of its true meaning. May the way of these teachings be made straight without derision, lest it impune a Higher Authority.

Nothing is ever known until it is first a question in the mind. A noble quest for each ion of Truth. The format of the following text is therefore written in question and answer form. If a question cannot be answered on a single page it becomes the boorish literature of theological discussion designed more to persuade than to instruct.

Time and the Word Machine

Part I

The Story of Consciousness

Life Model

1

What Is Life?

Life is not complex. Life is not complicated. Life is the doorway of experience of all that is Absolute.

The Absolute is anything which is infinite or is eternal.

There are only two absolutes in the world, Truth is infinite and Love is eternal.

Life is the Love of truth, therefore, Life is both infinite and eternal.

Life is the only quality that is both infinite and eternal.

2

How Does Life Begin?

Life is the coming from darkness into greater Light.

Life is a lion rampant, the knightly poise of singular Purpose.

The singular Purpose of Life is to place all discursive Medusa thought upon the straightened path of the Aesculapius rod and in this manner give Purpose to all meaning in Life such that we are truly Alive.

In Wisdom ask in Virtue give

3

How Is Life Given to the Name?

The Name is a developing word. The Name is the eye that cannot see itself. The Name is but a simple reflection (n-1) of the infinite meaning (n) of the 1 singular Purpose 'to be'.

In the Nordic system, in the beginning time only Lif (Life) is present within the seed of deity (two) and it brings forth triunal Being that is sustained by Matriarchal Faith, which is the lion's courage that looks ever eastward into the rising sun.

All else is brought to bear upon the visage of the South. This is the worldly awakening beauty of the morning sky and the dawn of the morning Light, and the opening beauty of the Lotus.

4

How Is Life Given?

It is given as a Word Name and is baptized in the Perfect Image possessing the Highest Expression of Freedom that is set forth as a strong body and healthy mind that being together are much like a precious stone keenly placed and well set upon the Pommel of Life (Lif).

And yet in that instant place between the grip and the blade is the guardian quillon of protective careful heed in every decision (God's scission) that is in constant contact within the instant of singular Purpose of Being that is struck acutely upon the holomorphic path of every thoughtful moment.

The Name is a place where all meaning lay in infinite award of every word, wherein rests the true value of the Sword of Power (Intellect).

In every inquiry made within the *Intellect* there is an Asking that gathers words into the developing power of meaning within the mind and its pictured form is Emblazoned by Imagination (Imagization) as a Word-Picture. The Intellect and the Imagination are the elements of Desire.

In the beginning always Ask and in that instant all is Emblazoned. Ask and Embla are the children of Alfadr upon the First Path and Lif is ever present.

Time Model

5

What Is Time?

The answer is simple.

Time is a measurement of separation.

Do not be confused by the complexity of a more definitive answer which defines time in terms of its measurement as an expenditure—as a duration of quantum occurrence.

6

What Is the Chaldean Word-line?

The most ancient paradigmatic example of consciousness and the intervening exclusionary moment of evolving time are present within the Chaldean word-line.

The Chaldean word-line comprises a straight line drawn between 2 points.

The first point is called Purpose and the second point is called meaning. Purpose and meaning are in every word.

The Chaldean word-line is the ancient description of the Aesculapius rod supporting the serpent's straightened path giving Truth to meaning and giving back Life.

Apollo slew Python, but Aesculapius, the son of Apollo, did not slay the serpent but gave it Life upon the straightened path of Truth. Life is the Love of Truth. Of all the gods, only Aesculapius could give back Life.

7

When Did Time First Occur?

Because Time is a creation and all things are created by words, Time did not occur until the First Word occurred.

Time is born of Grace (Principle of time) and came into Being with the First Word long ago in the beginning Millennium of ancient Ur.

8

What Is the First Word?

The First Word is Peace—Shalom alekhem, the nature of goodness in mankind, the Spirit of Islam.

Peace came into Being in Truth's Absolute obeyance with the perfect order of tranquility in the universe.

9

What Are the Adjective Elements Which Define the Chaldean Word-line?

The Chaldean Word-line is an algorithmic picture form of the Word.

All words are comprised of the linear joined adjective equivalent elements of Purpose and meaning. The allegoristic geometric form of words is constructed as points at each end of the same line.

This is the basic form of the Chaldean Word-line. There is only one universal purpose aligned with the infinite array of meaning.

The Purpose of every word is the same but the meaning of every word is different. Purpose is unity and meaning is infinity and they are both upon the same line. Meaning is the nexus of words, and Purpose is the unity of words, the unification of all creation. All is in all in meaning, all is made whole in Purpose.

The governing mode of resonant intent of every word resounds upon the sounding board of singular Purposeful harmonic echoed count of responsive linear strands within an endless reoccurring matrix of vibratory substance of First

Path meaning within the singular creative instant 'to be', that in separate order becomes the mechanical elements of time between words.

10

Where Is the Instant Found?

The instant is the center of the word-line, the fulcrum point of all Being that teeters in balance in the timeless moment when the derivation of Purpose first touches meaning.

We lift our cups to Urth in memory of Auld-Lang-Syne, of old times long past, and we in token words, toast to the future of Skuld. But wherein does Verdande, keeper of the present instant, set his feet in joyful comradeship between what is past and what will occur in the future?

When the past is ended the future begins, where is the present moment to be found? Is it found in the future of Skuld or in the past of Urth?

We are timeless travellers and live within the instant of each word and move effortlessly upon the slope of the derivative line of each directed thought.

We enjoy adventure within the timely moment of separation between words that lay upon our path of knowing within each moment of Grace.

11

How Many Instants Are There in Time?

There is but one instant in the universe and it is in the Name. And even though there may be many meanings there is but one Name.

The Name holds all meaning.

For the sake of eternity (for goodness' sake), do not strike against meaning within a word, it serves no Purpose. Weakness always strikes against strength. Remember always (All-paths) there is only goodness.

The instant of all words becomes the singular Purposeful meaning in the final moment of the word 'TO BE.'

All meaning that enters into the worldly-word of our Name in the Becoming 'WILL BE THAT WHICH IS.' Will become our re-word (reward), the place of our word at the time of Ragnarok, the end of time.

All light enters within Darkness from without is but the beginning path into greater Light, and All is in All in our Name in the instant moment.

This is the great burst of Light, the new moment (Nova) when all is made whole again. That is celebrated on November 1st, called the "first fire of Bel."

12

What Is the Element of Discernment Which We Call Knowing?

Knowing is the instantaneous moment when Purpose touches meaning within the word-line. Knowing is the fulcrum point of the word and occurs within the instant.

Perception is the knowing of the interrelated meaning between two or more words and it occurs in time as Understanding of summational meaning of what is known.

Knowing is the instantaneous Gestalt knowledge that disappears in Time to become Understanding that is eternal.

Understanding and Faith are the inseparable gendered qualities of the human Being. They are the qualities of the Spiritual nature of mankind.

13

What Is the Difference between Knowing and Learning?

Knowing occurs in the instant within the word. Learning occurs in time between the intervening space between words.

Learning and knowing are most often linked to a single event in which both occur in reciprocative procession.

Knowing instinctively without a preceding learning process is intuitive and increases with experience.

14

How Is Time Related to the Word-line?

Time is the separation between the meanings of 2 word-lines and their determinant form touching at the instant intercept to produce the 3rd word of meaning in Grace, which enters as power into the Name.

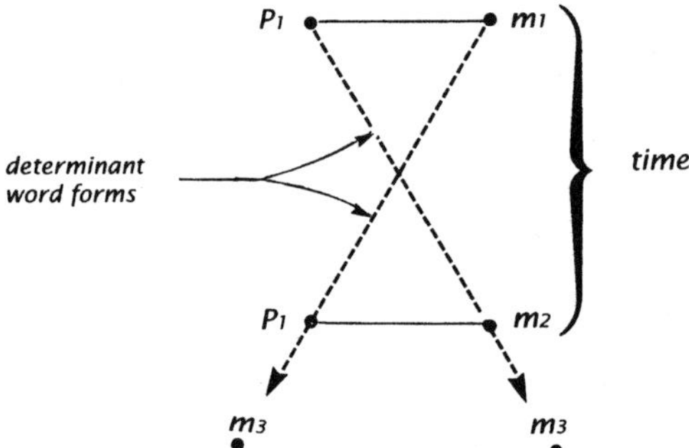

Chaos occurs as the disordered separation of words. The disorder of words not yet bound in Asking is ignorance, which is called Ginnungagap, the great yawning space of the premundane abyss of words that revolve in chaos as the formless void of the unconnected instant of words within the Name.

15

How Does the Name Interact and Change with Conscious Being?

Consciousness occurs in time between words as the joined perception of each instant.

Consciousness is the knowing path of each instant. This is the path of the Timeless Traveller in thought.

Within the infinite number of word meanings (n) our Name, which is designated as being apart from the whole (n-1), is a beginning word-line structure that cannot see itself since all visualization is by reflection.

Our Name (n-1) is the unitary holding power of the negative sign placed on (-1) that is juxtapositioned within the perfect order of the Mneme and is always potentially pending in the mysterious quadratic materialization of Desire.

The Name is the Asking word-line structure of the square surface Emblazonment of Alfadr (see pg. 54) Emblematically seen as the square base of the pyramid. Its extracted root is ($\sqrt{-1}$), an imaginary reversal of conception and perceived as an irrational function of an infinite set of words.

Meaning within the word is perceived by reflection and time by abstract absorption of the instant by the Name and all begins again.

Reflected meaning and the absorbed instant are perceived (perhaps) as induced substance within the empty matrix of timeless space (see pg. 35) as subatomic particles that fill the eight empty spaces of the matrix.

16

How Is Consciousness Mathematically Defined Relative to the Name?

Consciousness is mathematically defined as the unity of Purpose and the infinite nature of meaning within the structure of the word-line.

$$consciousness = \sum_{1}^{\infty} word = Name = (n\text{-}1)$$

This expression is only true for the instant of knowing. In general, within the timely learning process, which is sometimes called the Becoming, consciousness is set between limits → in meaning and only begins to become expansive during the quickening as a timeless acceleration of knowing. Knowing is the power of the instant within the word. This is the power that enters the Name.

Thought is the vehicle of eternity formed of two words that carries the divine Triunal Principle of a third word as knowledge which is called understanding, into the Name The Name is the Soul of Being.

Life's → Purpose → of Being

The Quickening is the approaching integral of timelessness in knowing in Harmony and Life begins again upon a higher plateau of knowing. Life, Purpose, and Being are the first three Truths in the hierarchy of Truths which are found in the First Bough of the Tree of the World and they also comprise the three words in the first vertical row of the Ennead (as shown on pg. 32).

17

What Is Grace?

When all is in all, there is not separation and time is made whole, a condition which the ancients called Grace.

Grace is the Principle of time which embodies all eternity, and each lifetime is defined as a single moment of Grace, a single segment of time.

When meaning becomes all that is in all Purpose is made whole and Life is complete in the word-line of the Name, and the moment of Grace ends—we have become the power of our Word.

18

How Was Deity First Recognized and Symbolically Represented?

Deity (duality) is unity in masculine and feminine thought and most generally represented by the symbol of the Anka in Heaven.

When deity enters creation it enters time and is separated into gender as man and woman and this is symbolized by the scarab.

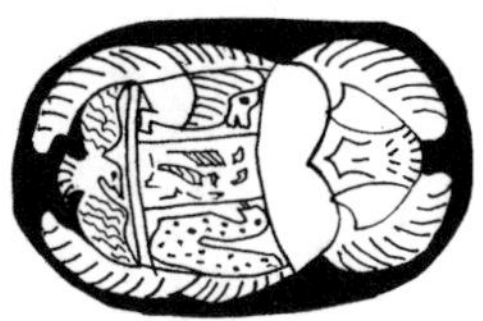

The duality of thought is represented by geometric structure as perpendicularity, parallelity, and angularity. In

gendered triunal closure they represent the mutual perpendicularity, trestled (bridged) parallelity, and fixed structure
(immovable) principle as triangularity.

19

What Is the Becoming?

When the instant of the final word is absorbed in the Name we become all that is in all and our Purpose is made whole and Life is complete.

In the Nordic belief this is the time of Ragnarok, when all is destroyed and only Life (Lif) remains as the power in the word that once more passes from deity into gendered Being as Ask and Embla, the beginning place of all creation.

20

Conclusion

Words are the grazing substance of thought, the graminae of preceding knowledge.

Arranged in sentence structure, words are categorized as nouns, pronouns, adjectives, verbs, adverbs, prepositions, conjunctions, interjections and in general arrangement as assembled elements of syntax of what is conveyed as subject and predicate. But these are merely grammatical rules of usage and say nothing of the interior workings of the word.

The exterior elements of syntactical usage of words address the time-dependent mnemonic character of learning, but the interior elements of the word address the timeless instant of knowing, the Gestalt nature of Being not yet given Purpose, this is the path of the timeless traveler.

The distinctive elements of gender found in other rhetorical systems reflect the continuing need of deity. Although most plaudable in this Desire, deity cannot exist in time, it must inherit the word, which the ancients referred to as the kingdom of God. Thus is the plight of Hermes made apparent.

True knighthood, most honorable in its quest for deity need only enoble thought and deed to set forth and to seek and find the holy grail of meaning in words.

There is a cryptographic element within every word. Each word stands on the strength of its own discernment and each word to be fully understood must enter the mind

and experience the devotion and love of its own Being. As
we are taught as children the Word, the World and the Intellect which is called the Sword-of-Power gathers
all-that-is-in-all.

Word
wor-l-d
S-word

I will speak no more of this word-ship lest it wor-ray
emerging privilege of knowing in thought.

Thought Model

The thought model employs the elements of the Chaldean Word-line in conjunction with the Ennead to produce new words and thoughts.

21

What Is Thought?

Thought is the joining of two words. Each word holds the timeless instant at its center but each is separate and is joined in thought in the instant moment of beginning Grace.

What Is Idea?

Idea is the God within. Ideas are formed in Grace (time) by two or more thoughts.

What Is a Concept?

Concepts are formed by two or more Ideas. Concepts are the conceptual substance of all Creation existing in Grace (time).

What Is a System?

Systems are formed by two or more concepts as in the instance of joining two or more subjects gathered in independent sentence structure supporting a common belief. Creation is comprised of two or more systems.

22

What Is a Word-line Intercept?

The point at which two word-lines cross is called an intercept, meaning internal conception.

The point of the word-line intercept is infinitely small, it is without area or volume and therefore it does not exist, it is only extant beyond time, existing within the in-stant. The point is intent existing within the context of the instant. Because it exists within the instant of the word it is conceived inwardly, it is an inception of the intercept of two words.

Word-lines are always straight, there is no curvature in word-line construction. Curvature occurs as an infinitely changing slope ($\frac{dy}{dx}$) of changing inclination and declination of an infinite number of word-line determinates joined in series.

$$(P_1 + m_1)\,(P_2 + m_2) - - - - - - - - -(P_n + m_n)$$

When the slope of the construction of the determinate between two or more word-lines is positive the generated thought is ascending, when the slope of the determinate is negative the thought is descending.

All words have a common unit value in Purpose and also carry potential infinite meaning within an expanding numerical order in their Ogdoad formulation. Where there is both unit value and set unit order, predictability of thought is possible by matrix determinate resolution, thereby indicating a prefunctionary perception of obscure meaning in theory but reassembled as a mathematical system of artificial intelligence.

23

What Is Conation?

Conation comprises the three conjunctive elements that join Volition → Desire → Will, into a single determinant form which changes Purpose into etymological intent in the generated form of a third word (m_3) within the continuum of the developing word.

The third word is called the derivative ($\frac{dy}{dx}$) of Purpose with respect to its determinant formative meaning (m_3).

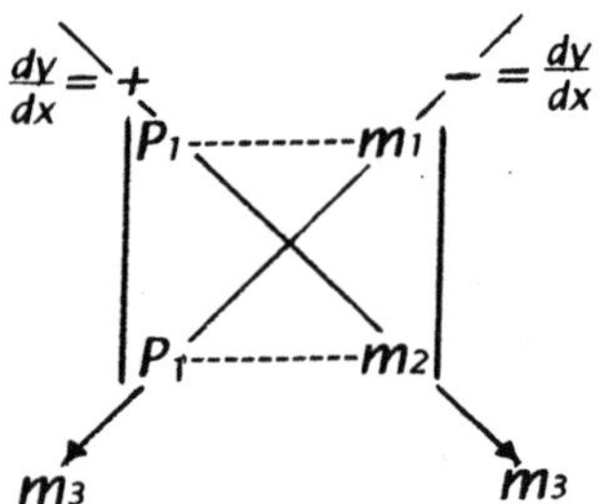

Volition is the instant point between Purpose and Grace in the Ennead which is also called the Grail. This is the Word-Machine that generates all thought.

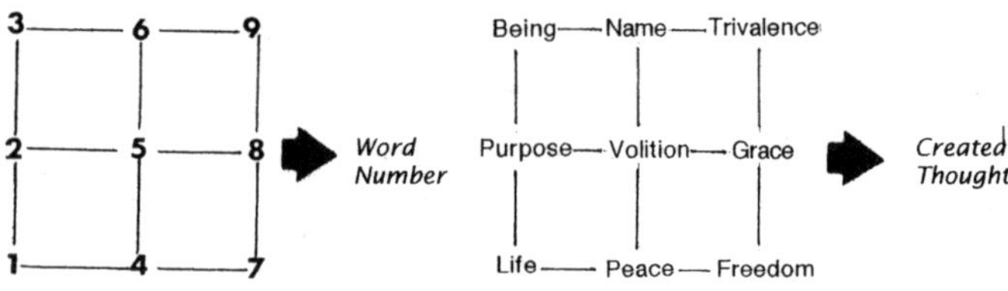

The nine points of Heindahl's lens are the nine strings of Scota's harp which are called Netters, which comprise the nine points of the Netters grid which is called the Ennead.

24

What Is the Holy Grail?

The Grail is a cooking and serving platter, a flat plate utensil configured and fashioned in a grid-like form that is employed during the final service of the Tarquinian sacrificial ceremony to cook and to serve the final sacraments from the altar flame. This is the last supplement of the ceremonial procedure following the Sanguine libation from the Golden Chalice.

The Holy Grail is the Ennead.

The Chaldean word-line in the creation of the materia prima in the form of the carbonaceous tetrahedron and in the form of the development of the pyramid have in the dim light of unwritten history become an object of interest in the study of the Eucharist in the celebration of transubstantiation.

25

What Is Timeless Space?

Most generally all three-dimensional elements having length, width, and height, constitute a volume and volumes always create space and encompass an element of separation.

Truth is infinite, but Truth is also the culmination of all time.

In the logic of geometrical reasoning Truth is the intersecting point (coincident point) of the perpendicular between two word-lines and there is no separation.

Only three mutually perpendicular lines can be drawn through a single point.

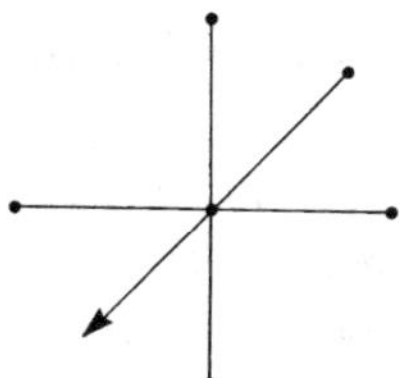

Time is a measure of separations. Three mutually perpendicular lines passing through a common point are not separate in their ogdoad formation of the light open quadrants enveloping the timeless single intercepting point in meaningless three dimensions. This is the high potential of beginning Purpose in volitional assembly of meaning in word structure.

26

How Many Types of Thought Occur in the Mind?

There are three types of thought, they are categorized as:

- Coincident thought (Truth)
- Directed thought (Words)
- Fixed thought (Principles).

In geometric word-form thoughts are evolved as:

1. perpendicularities as Truth
2. parallities as Words
3. and triangularities as Principles.

Thought-form begins as two word-lines. Each distinctive third word characterizes the combined meaning as the derivative of thought. The derivative words are also called determinates.

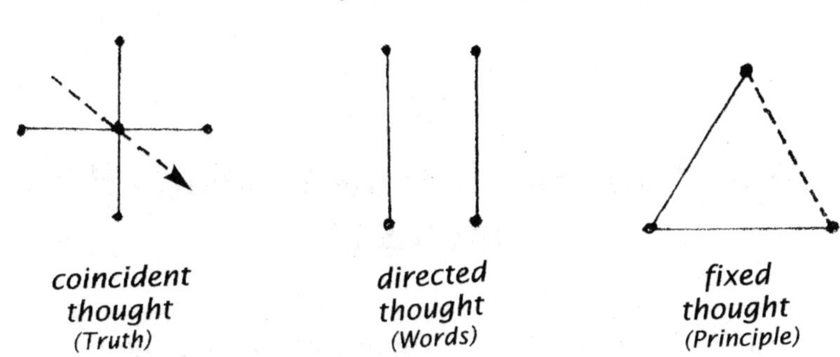

Deific word-line transition to Triadic Thought

27

How Did the Ancients Envision the Intellect?

The intellect was called the Sword of Power, the cutting edge of all societal progress and Spiritual development, which was seen to occur in many of the most ancient emerging cultures as a great battle fought upon a Martian plain of human endeavor. A great battle that was fraught with many dangers and adversity of every kind, which could only end victoriously by constancy of the Word (Name) raised up in Asking (prayer) upon a higher plain of Spiritual belief.

All things are created by words in thought and by the infinitesimal naometry of the ogdoad material placed within the matrix of timeless space.

The duality of word-line in deity (2) interacts only in three ways. In perpendicular words intersecting at a point of destined commonality of Truth. In parallelism words are infinitely outward bound in pairs in singular Purpose and opposed; meaning in intensity to generate a third word in an upward bound transverse path (Hermes Path). The Purpose and meaning (proton and neutron) of timeless space become the outward bound path of all that Aphrodite creates.

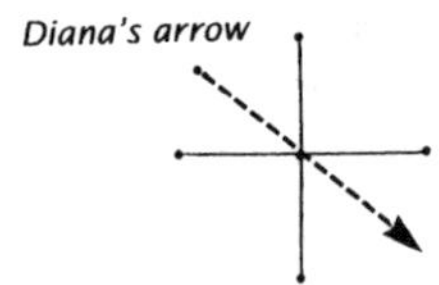

The longitudinal timeless matrix of the Aphrodite's purposeful path holds the cementing material substance of the eight quadrant operators of the Ogdoad of the Ennead in relative combination in correspondence of their finite timely destiny within the seven Boughs of the Tree of the World.

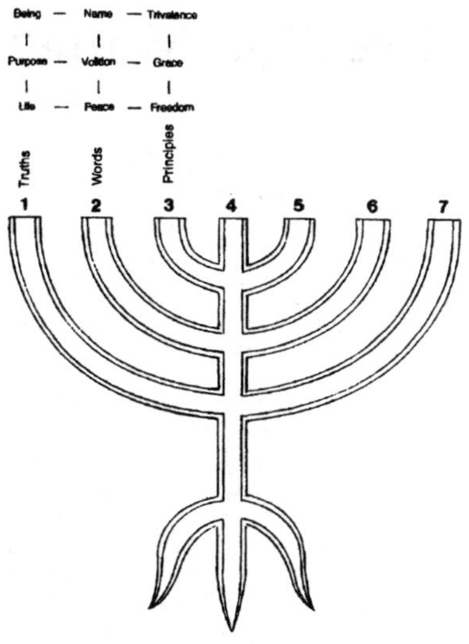

Creation Model

28

What Is Cosmogony?

Cosmogony is the story of Purpose, the beginning element of all meaning occurring in Grace within an extending separation of words, which is the modal substance of time in all that is to be.

Creation begins with the end of Ragnarok, the end of time, from the beginning form of thought to its dissolution and the rise of the gods from the smoke (rokr) and the beginning twilight of Ask and Embla (Adam and Eve) and the emergence of Lif (Life) within the cyclic process, the time when all mankind is born again in each moment of Grace, and Asks again in Desire (Deis-Sire) standing before the Oddin Bough (Odin), also called Alfadr, the center bough between heaven and earth and Embla emblazons all within the picture world created from the word.

29

What Is Meant by the Term Communicatio Ideomatum?

This is the doctrine of the two natures of mankind. The incorporeal divine Being and the corporeal human nature. Both impart their peculiar properties to the other in deity in heaven and in creation as gender. These are ascending and descending thought characteristics respectively.

The divine nature is the Hermetic substance that resides in the High Place (Ennead) and cannot descend. The human nature is the Aphrodite Spiritual Being that descends in gendered form and brings all life into the world. All other creation is but inanimate word-line construction that does not contain the Living Substance of Desire which is to say, Deis-Sire and therefore does not contain the seed of God the Father (Alfadr).

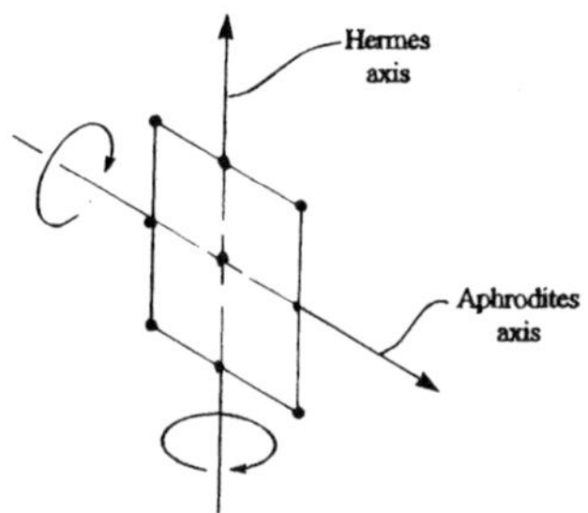

Hermes rises above time in Desire standing upon the square stone of eternity. Aphrodite carries both the purpose of Hermes Being and corporeal being into creation.

All inanimate creation is the product of chaotic unguided entropy of word-line assembly into three-dimensional form.

30

How Is the Desiderative Nature Numerically Represented and Geometrically Designated Symbolically by Word-line Structure?

Desideration is a conative line of force most generally represented as the intervening and pre-emptive element of Desire that is synchronically positioned between Volition and Will.

Volition → Desire → Will

Desire is numerically represented by the number 4 (fourth bough) and geometrically symbolized by the square formed by four word-lines.

Desire is called God-the-Father (Deis-Sire), the beginning seed of all creation. The square is a planar surface without a third dimensional element and therefore it is timeless.

It is the instant presence within the creative Word born of Asking and not yet Emblazoned in Purpose by Embla.

Ask and Embla are the two children that sit on each side of Odin who is called God-the-Father.

There is a third creative path (not shown) that is formed by the pentagonal structure of five equilateral triangles having linear elements that derive the Golden ratio that is found in plant life and in lower forms of vertebrate and invertebrate life.

31

What Is Life without Desire?

Life without Desire is the first possible word-line structure of volume which occurs as four triangular surfaces forming a tetrahedron which geometrically represents carbonaceous matter, the vital element of all corporeal substance which is set upon the First Path of the Perfect Image of Perfect Order of all Principle.

Tetrahedron

From the swirling void (nothingness), the dynamistic sustenance of the triunal presence of Principle is formed of the duality of deity (2) exhibiting the respective joined parallelity of the horizontal and vertical paths of Aphrodite and Hermes in which each stands in the collective Light of beginning consciousness in Desire.

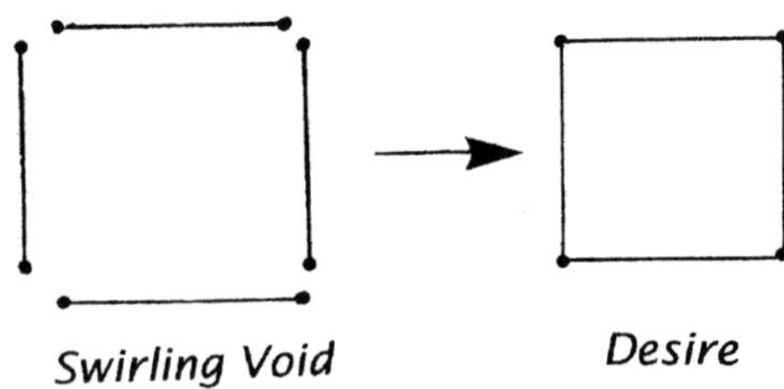

Swirling Void   *Desire*

When the four triangles of the tetrahedron are set lengthwise in serial union and then closed at their bottom line they form the square foundation base of the pyramid.

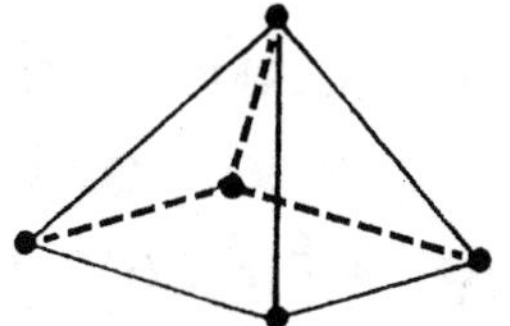

Pyramid (Fire within)

32

What Is Ragnarok and How Is It Related to "The Song of the Lord" and to the Day of Armageddon?

When meaning becomes all that is in all of our full enquiry then is Purpose made whole and Life is complete. This is the end of time, the joining moment of all words, and the instant coalesces (melds) with unity into the Name. This is the time of Ragnarok.

There is not good and evil in the world, only goodness. Neither is there friend and foe, only friendship. Words, misunderstanding between the friendship of families (Bhagavad Gita) as told in the Lord's harmonious Song of All that is in All.

Armageddon is mankind's great struggle to swim upstream and ascend to the spawning ground of words in the quiescent pond between Truth and Principle.

Eternity is given in Understanding between words in a moment of Grace and we are delivered from material bondage and begin our journey upon the Second Path standing in the Light of deity.

At the end of Ragnarok only Lif (Life) remains. Then at the door of appearance, Ask and Embla (Adam and Eve), the first gendered Beings, and the way is made straight upon the Path in Principle (Freedom).

The First Path begins with Lif, the First Truth. The Second Path begins with the First Principle, Freedom, and is forever and ever in infinite Being as the deity of Ask and Embla.

33

How Did Life First Progress from the Word?

In the beginning time of Ur it was taught that all corporeal life began as the progression of word-line structure which first evolved from the protoplasmic carbonaceous structure assembled in the beginning form of the tetrahedron.

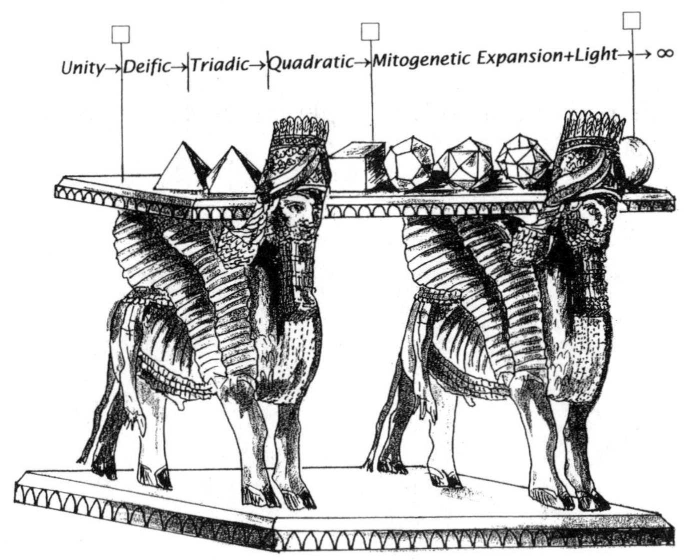

Geometric Word Expansion and Transmutation in the Name

The tetrahedron is the first possible three-dimensional structure to be evolved by word-line construction. But the tetrahedron does not possess the Seed of God the Father (Deis-Sire) in its beginning form, it did not possess the Spiritual element of Desire, the geometric form of the Square was not present.

Tetrahedron

Word-line Construction of the Four Surfaces of the Tetrahedron

All of life remained as simple corporeal substance without Desire.

34

How Was Incorporeal Spiritual Life Symbolically Evolved from Its Corporal Beginning?

A voice was heard. "Let us create Life from the seed of our own Image that it may know Spiritual Being."

Corporeal life begins as the formative world-line construction as four triangular surfaces in which each in their individual planar construction represent four separate fixed-thoughts (two-ideas) and each evolve as concepts in creation.

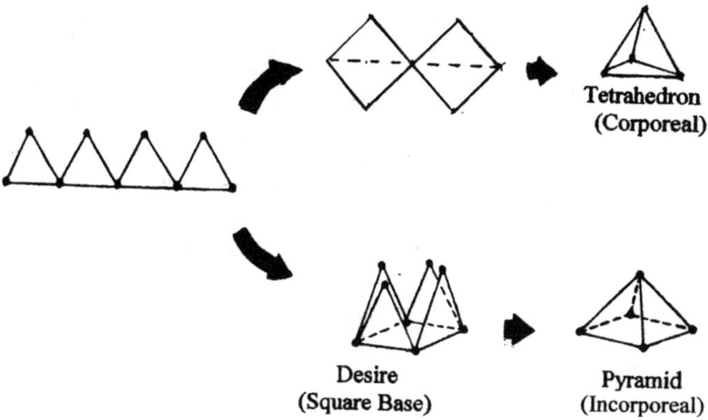

Transubstantiation—substance according to the same theory consists of two essential elements or principles, one passive and indifferent called the matter (materia prima) and the other active and determining called the substantial form. The matter is supposed to be the same in all bodies and the specific nature and characteristics of each one are determined by its form.

35

How Does Trilinear Word-line Triangular Surface Construction of Fixed-Thought Relate to Quadratic Square Surface Symbolism of Desire?

All word-lines are the same length and, therefore, inherent in their closed trilinear construction, form equilateral triangles. When the bases of the triangles are joined at right angles at each end, they enclose the quadratic square surface, the symbol of Desire. The synergistic combined interaction of each word-line of the square are the definitive elements of conative strength bridging the separative void between Volition and the Will. The remaining eight word-lines reach up to the Oddi (Old Norse, point) awaiting Closure in parallel word-line deity (two) in directed thought.

The evolution of the tetrahedron to the pyramidal form is the transmutation from the corporeal beginning form of living matter to the Spiritual Being occurring as the in-corporation of the Father's seed (Deis-Sire) Desire.

Because the corporeal and incorporeal originate from the same four Principles (triangles, fixed-thought) their volumes are related in the same manner.

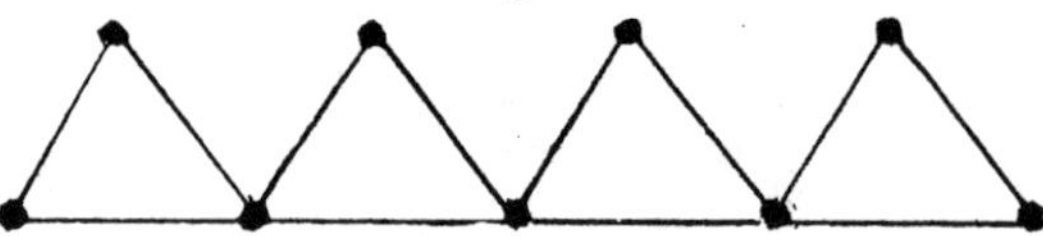

Linear Serial Alignment

But when the four triangles are arranged in a square the closed system generates a continuum of the Living Spirit in which the deity (doubling) their closed word-lines evolve as a pyramid.

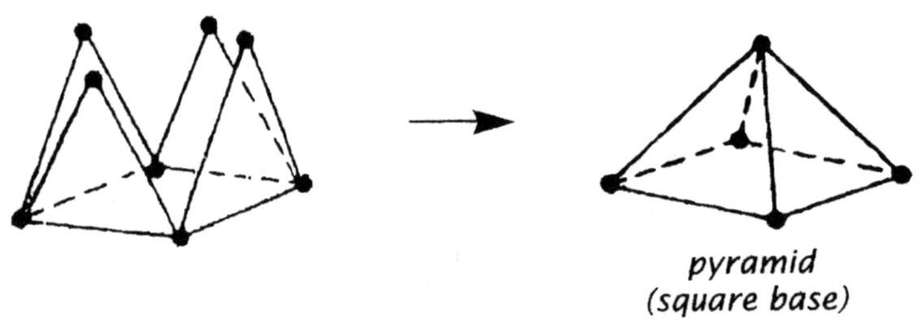

36

What Is the Relationship of Fixed-Thought (Triangulation) Principles in the Formation of the Tetrahedral Volume and That of the Pyramidal Volume?

Three word-line triangles form the tetrahedral volume between six word-line elements. Four word-line triangles form the pyramidal volume enclosed between twelve word-line elements which has the capability of expanding to the cubic volume of the Caba and this transmutation is likened in the Egyptian system to the awakening lotus in the coming quarter Light coming forth by day.

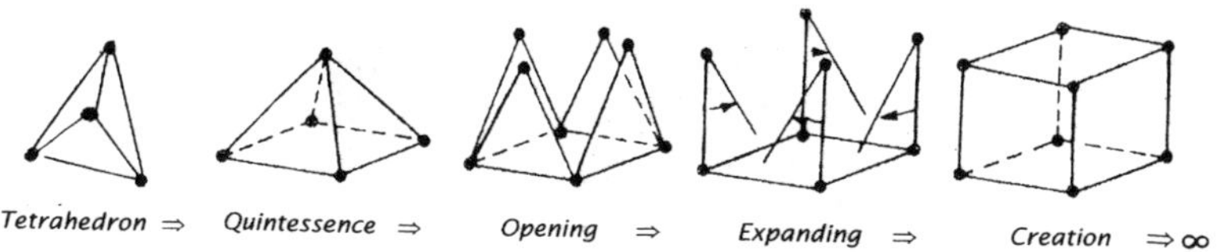

Surface to Volume Quadratic Word Expansion

When two diagonal corners of the Caba (cube) are pressed inward toward one another cubic volume disappears and the cross-section of the sphere becomes apparent as six triangles and these combine with continuing infinite triangulation and infinite rotation that forms the encirclement of all that is in all in all of eternal Grace. This is the secret of the squaring of the circle.

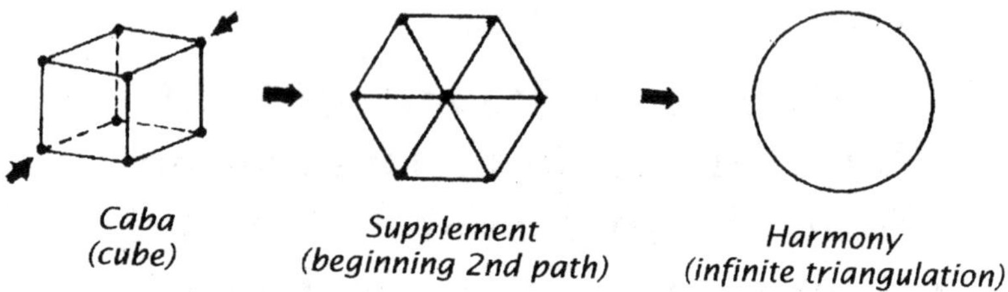

Caba
(cube)

Supplement
(beginning 2nd path)

Harmony
(infinite triangulation)

Cubic Dilation Relative to Time and Position

The six equilateral triangles are the twelve word-line final supplement of the first Path. These are the starting elements of the second Path, the beginning point of Harmony, the dwelling place of Peace and goodness in mankind which is called Islam.

37

What Are the Twelve Apostles of the Last Supplement of the Geometric Progression upon the First Path?

The twelve apostles are called the twelve witnesses of Volition within the Ennead. They are the twelve word-lines of the four equilateral triangles that form the edges of the tetrahedron. They are the same twelve word-lines which form the pyramid and the Caba. They are the same twelve word-lines that form the timeless planar cross-section of the sphere holding all-that-is-in-all in the unfolding lotus in the awakening light of beginning Harmony.

38

What Is Religion?

Religion is the Chaldean Word-line that denotes the connecting linear element that binds Purpose to meaning in words and by this anamnestic process creates all things.

The ancients called the word-line a ligament that binds Purpose to meaning. Therefore a word-line is a ligament within a single word, a binding element. Re-ligion denotes a rebinding of Purpose to meaning.

The anamnestic process is the Mneme of mankind, the memory of mankind in Creation and the order of Being in Heaven.

Religion provides the primeval elements of modern vibrating string theory that joins all meaning in a continuum of Harmony in unification in Purpose.

Part II

The Tree of the World

The Tree of the World Model
A Study of the Bicameral Nature of Consciousness

39

What Is the Tree of the World?

The Tree of the World is a memory Tree, a Mnemonic instrument, which in its pictured form is a map denoting every place where the mind may journey.

There is a certain privileged knowledge, which by its understanding can lift the comprehension of even the most primitive mind far above that of an accomplished scholar. The privileged knowledge is the teaching of the Tree of the World, which is the second teaching of the Quadriga.

The word-picture of its descriptive text forms the arborescent structure found in nature as it relates to the epistemic growth of the human mind. It describes the cybernetic linkage of the thought process that occurs between Purpose and meaning and its numerical concept to tangible form for those who cannot read or write.

But this teaching is much more than a mere perfunctory exercise to lessen the mnemonic burden of rote learning. It is the teaching of the two minds, the mind in Heaven that knows the unity of Truth, the deity of words, and the Trivalence of Principle, and the mind in the Garden Paradise that knows the Quintessent purity of the five senses in Creation that are in Harmony with all Being.

40

What Is the Bicameral Mind?

From the earliest times mankind has sought to explain the bicameral nature of their own Being in precise individual terms that will permit the separate definitive study of each half without the distractive attending duality of the descriptive nature and influence of the other.

The dividing point of the two minds is the juncture where deity enters consciousness in gendered form to separate in time.

The bifurcation of this duality is always at the juncture of the word <u>THE.</u>

The sacred and the profane
The Spiritual and the temporal
The incorporeal and the corporeal
The clerical and the secular

Standing at the juncture of individual development and disjointment of the mental and material substance one finds the natural path of Spiritual discernment in the study of <u>THE</u>ology upon the garden path or in the field of nature within the scientific principles of <u>THE</u>ory.

But the perception of these qualities always begins in the same manner.

First the Word, then
the picture, then

the number and its unit order

    And all is made whole again in the singular equation of
Life.

41

How Is the Tree of the World Related to the Game of Chess?

The Tree of the World and the game of chess both reflect and relate the duality of the mind in context with established Being.

Only a special few know that the Tree of the World is the matrix board of the elements of the chess pieces of the two kingdoms of mankind. The two castles are the two minds. The two knights are the noble endeavor in each mind. The two bishops are the omnipresence of the Spiritual Being in both mindly kingdoms. The king and the queen are the unity and infinity of the joined deity of Truth and love. The king is the most important and weakest piece on the board, and the queen in Purpose holds the Seed of the eternal nature of mankind. The queen is the most powerful piece on the board for only she can give the Seed its Life and bring it Alive into the Second Kingdom in gendered time. But of the many few born equal of the eternal nature of Being only the pawn of mankind can raise itself to become all things in all places of its own choosing. It is the Mutative Will to be born again upon the infinite path of the Timeless Traveller. It is a secret well known.

The Tree of the World is an idiometer of oneself in knightly quest of Life's singular Purpose 'to be'.

42

Who Were the Tree Knowers of the Northern Nations?

The Teutonic peoples, those who worshipped Teutates, were the Tree Knowers. The Northern Tree is a conifer having a pointed center bough which the Norse people called the Oddi. This was the Oddin Bough, which later became the residence of Odin, called Alfadr, and later God-the-Father, Deis-sire.

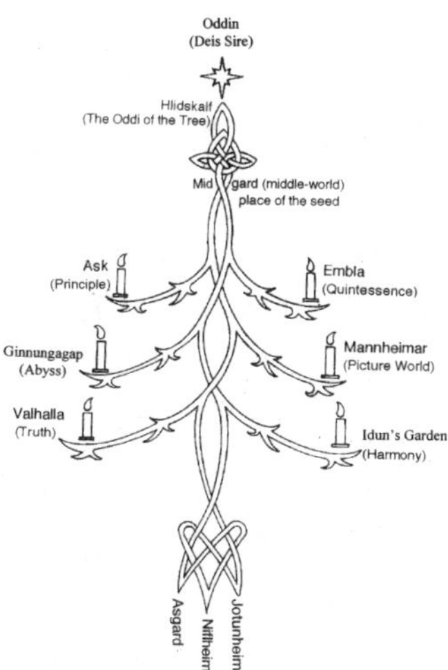

During the era of the Frankish monarchies much of this early lore of the Tannenbaum was lost. Today the Tree is cel-

ebrated during the Yule months and is often referred to as
the Yule Tree. The early Tannenbaum served the same function of the Egyptian Opet celebration and the early Roman
Saturnalia and in active contrast serves the same ceremonial
role as the five great stone triliths that stand in the center of
Stonehenge.

43

Is the Conative Force That Emanates from the Oddi an Ascending Force or Is It a Descending Force?

The conative force of the Oddin Bough is both ascending and descending. Odin who is sometimes referred to as God-the-Father, or simply Deis-Sire, and at other times as Alfadr, who by his conative seed creates all things through six Desires, three ascending and three descending in determinate signed value.

The emanation of the Oddi is the Light of the guiding star that radiates infinite meaning into Creation and Unity into Being.

Mankind has only six Desires, three happinesses and three vital imperatives. The three happinesses are pleasure, delight and joy, which in bliss are an ascending presence. The three vital imperatives are descending elements that pass into Creation within each moment of Grace. They are conception, sustainment and a protective element of human behavior.

44

Where Can the Tannenbaum
Be Seen Today?

The Tannenbaum can be seen in the Holy of Holies in the temple of Diana on the island of Rhodes in the eastern Mediterranean.

The temple of Diana is a temple of baptism, a place where power first comes into the Name.

The Name is the only word that cannot see itself because it cannot reflect light from its inner source so it is the only word that need be baptised.

When Alexander visited the island and helped repair the temple he requested that his Name be placed on the foundation stone. His request was denied by the temple priest with the simple explanation:

"One temple—one Name."

This reply was to emphasize that our Name is the temple of our Word.

45

How Is the Tree of the World Variously Described in Other World Cultures?

The Tree of the World is also called the Tree of Life and the Tree of Knowledge. In the northern nations, the Tree of the World is the tall, pointed conifer called the Tannenbaum tree. In the eastern nations, the Tree of the World is the yew tree and in biblical text, it is the apple tree. The Tree of the World symbolically represents the three dynamic principles of Force → Strength → Power that representatively reside in the static structure of the roots, trunk, and boughs. It is interesting to note that the ogdoad elements of the seven boughs of the Tree of the World may be analogous with the seven groups of the Periodic Table. The zero group of the table, representing the noble gases, is completely unreactive and seems to correspond to the unchanging Forces of the three great roots of the Tree.

Force is in the roots, strength is in the trunk and power is in its seven boughs.

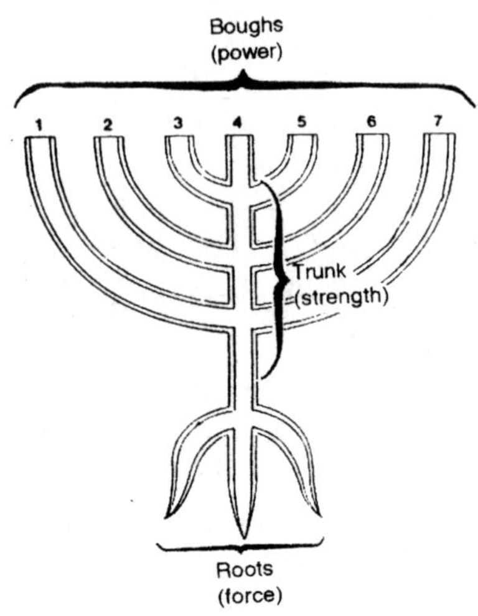

Boughs
(power)
1 2 3 4 5 6 7
Trunk
(strength)
Roots
(force)

46

Who Is Esus?

Esus is a Celtic Carpenter who built all things from the wood of the Tree of the World.

Carpenter is a Celtic word meaning Car-builder. The car is the chariot that carries the Spirit of mankind across the sky and over the Oddi of the Tree. This was the beginning time of the Apollo myth, and the ancient Essenian belief in the pinnacle Light and divine purity of all Creation.

Esus

47

How Are the Seven Boughs of the Tree of the World Related to the Seven Days of the Week?

The first day of the week is the sun's day and the second day is the moon's day, and the third day is the day of the principle of deity called Teutates' day. The fourth day is the mid-week day (Mittwock), it is the middle bough, the Oddin bough, it is the joining bough of heaven and earth, the wedding bough.

Because it is both Odin's bough and the wedding bough (Wednesday), it is also called Woden's Bough, a compromise word. The fifth bough is the purity bough, the Quintessent bough of the five senses. The sixth bough is the creation bough, the six square surfaces of the Caba, the six Deis-sires of mankind. The seventh bough is Saturn's bough, the Sabbath day when the moment of Grace expires and all time ends.

Ascending Triad
(kingdom of Teutates)
Descending Triad
(kingdom of Taranis)
1 2 3 4 5 6 7
Oddi
Midgard
Three points
of Excellence
Hidden Triad
(home of Cernunnos)
Asgard
Niflheim
Jotunheim
Golden Triad

Old

Mystical Boughs
Kingdom of Teutates
(Subjective mind)
Mythical Boughs
Kingdom of Taranis
(Objective mind)
First Truth
First Word
First Principle
Desire
Quintessence
Creation
Harmony
Intuition
Imagination
1 2 3 4 5 6 7
Scholars Point
(physical)
Philosophers Point
(intellectual)
Godly Point
(Spiritual)

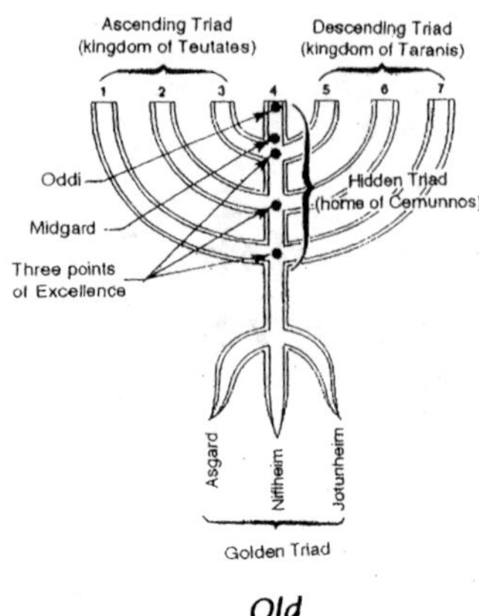

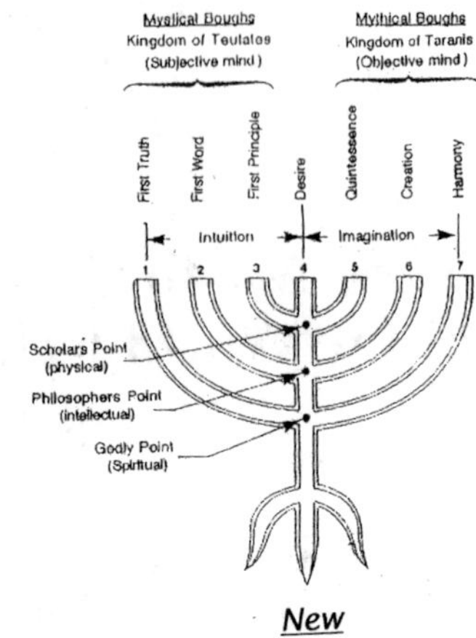

New

48

How Is the Bicameral Mind Related to the Three Divisions of the Tree?

The first division is the ascended elements that give Life. The center division is the Living Spirit that joins that which gives Life to the third division, which is the descended division, which receives Life and is Alive.

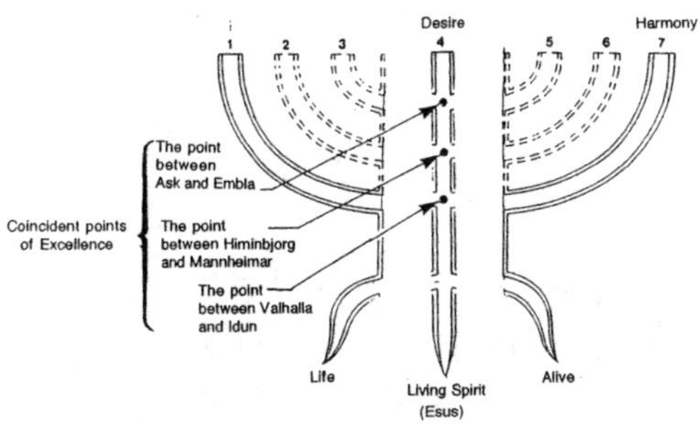

The seven rays of the crown of liberty are the glorious seven emanations of the seven boughs of the Tree of the World, the Seven beams of the Spirit beacon that lights the path of all mankind. How else shall one pass from liberty (Freedom) into Harmony and return again to Life?

That which gives Life, that which receives Life and is Alive, and the Living Spirit of Esus is All-that-is-in-All.

49

How Is Matter Created?

Matter is created and begins its timely moment at the coincident point of Purpose of all substantive subatomic nano particles that enter within the ogdoad vacant quadrants of the matrix of timeless space.

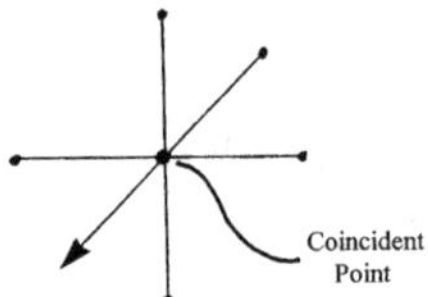

Matter is created in time as the separate ionic material of each of the seven boughs of the Tree of the World, each of which are subject to operative formational functions of the eight points of the Ennead.

The nucleus of the word is like the atomic model containing a neutron and a proton reacting overtly in time as subatomic nano particles of meaning and subscribed Purpose in the same respective manner.

All creation occurs in time within the matrix, and thus particles have both beginning and ending. All begins with Lif and ends in Ragnarok.

Timeless space is the Aphrodite's beginning Purpose attaining the seven qualities of the seven boughs of the Tree of the World each bough responding in the gentle order of the zephyr's pulse of the nine operative winds of time, each defined numerically as the occurrence with the word-number emanating from Being into the Principle of Grace (time).

50

How Is the Tree of the World Most Generally Observed Today?

In heaven our Word walks between Truth and Principle and we walk in the beauty of Creation between purity and harmony in Idun's Garden. But always within the radiant torc of goodness which spans each moment of Grace between Life and Harmony.

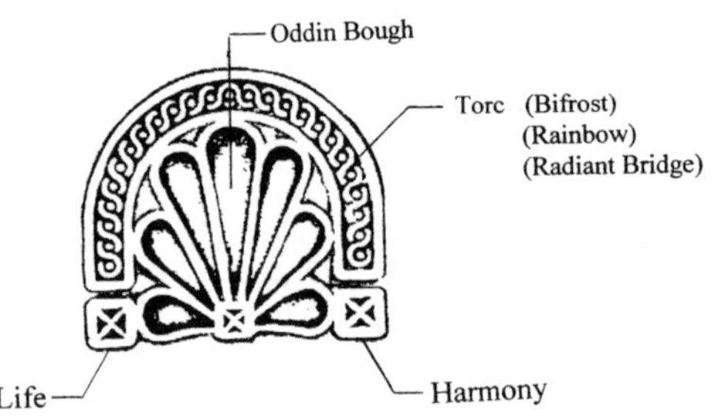

The Tree, the tre, the three parts of conscious Being that is born of Truth (Purpose) and Lives in the beauty of Idun's Garden (Harmony), always in the presence of Freyja (Freya), and with the loss of Frey (Fritag, Time) Freyja returns to Harmony on Saturn's day and all is made whole again and all time ends and there is not separation.

Gather to yourself the glorious bounty that awaits all mankind.

Part III

The Story of Stonehenge

Stonehenge Model
The Calendar Stones of Both Kingdoms

51

Who Built Stonehenge?

Stonehenge was built by the early Neolithic people of Britain.

Before the first millennium Britain was overrun by the Celtic tribes migrating from the east from the Aryan Uzbek and Turkmen regions in their final westward expansion to the channel coastline and along the Iberian peninsula. In their first contact with the Britons the Celtic warriors considered their speech excessively religious, full of thees and thous, much like the modern day Quakers and Amish people. For this reason they called them God-speaking or Deis-rouyd, which in its contracted form in later years became the word Druid.

Stonehenge was built by the aboriginal people of Britain and in later years the keepers of these early holy sites and establishments became known as Druids and the custom still remains.

52

How Many Moons Are There in One Year and How Many Days Are There in One Moon?

There are twelve moons in one year, thirteen new moons in a year, but the first and last new moon are the same moon. There are thirty days in each moon (month) such that there are only 360 days in a year.

$$12 \text{ moons} \times 30 \text{ days/moon} = 360 \text{ days}$$

The thirty days of each moon (month) are the thirty stones in the outer circle of Stonehenge. Each of the thirty stones is capped with a lintel stone such that the thirty upright stones each form a gate for each day of the month.

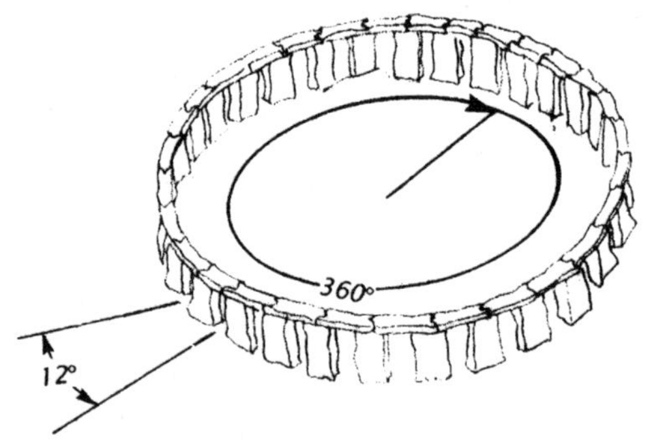

Each of the 360 days in the year represents one degree of radial arc (arch) within a full circle. Because it is generally assumed that the outer circle is fully developed by the thirty gates it has become customary to assume that each month represents 1/12 degree of complete rotation such that the total angular rotation of a circle is 360°.

30 gates x 12 degrees = 360°

53

Why Did the Celtic People Believe There Were Only 360 Days in the Year, When In Fact There Are 365?

There are thirty days in a moon (month) and yet it requires 365 days for the earth to complete one revolution about the sun.

There are only thirty gates in the circle, therefore five extra gates in the form of triliths were placed in the hollow of the outer circle. These five inner gates are the hollow gates which comprise the five holidays of the year.

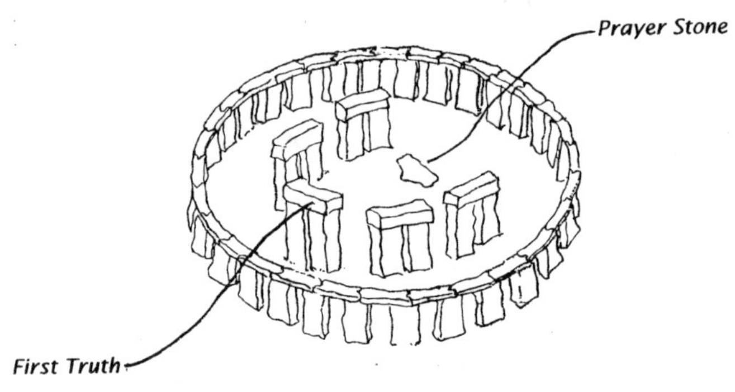

The five holidays lengthen the period extending from December 25th to the New Year's day, January 1st and they comprise the Yule Tide season of celebration.

54

What Do the Five Triliths That Are Placed in the Hollow of the Great Stone Circle Represent?

The five triliths in the hollow of the great stone circle represent the five additional gates upon the path of time necessary to bring closure to the year (360 + 5 = 365 days). Because they sit in the center hollow of the circle they are called Hollow-days which have come to be known as holidays representing the elapsed period of time extending between Yuletide (December 25) to the beginning of the first day of the new year (January 1) which is called the Janus day because it can see both the beginning and the end, the new and the old. Closure is brought into Being by Quintessence in belief (Faith) and all is made whole in creation, and nothing else of Osirian generative principle need be added.

55

How Are the Five Center Triliths Positioned in the Hollow of the Circle?

The five triliths representing the gates of the five holidays are positioned in a horseshoe pattern within the outer circle of gates.

The two sides of the horseshoe form the individual Matriarchal and Patriarchal paths which merge at the center trilith which is the largest of the five triliths is the center trilith and is called the First Truth because it represents the three absolute qualities of Spirituality on both the Patriarchal and Matriarchal path.

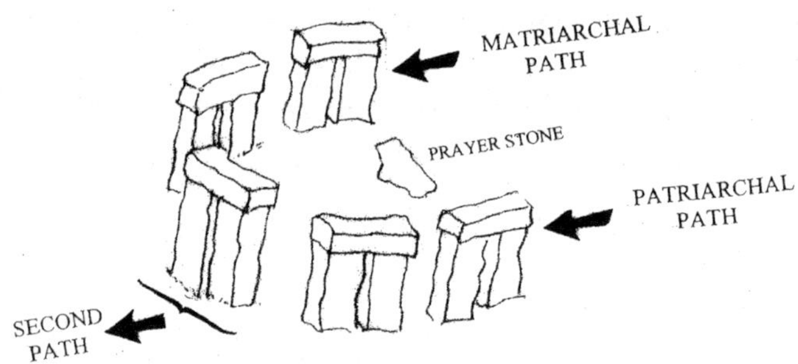

The Matriarchal path is the path of Embla and therefore is said to sit at the Right hand of Deis because it possesses in its unity the Principle of Trinity and Faith. Trinity is the Father, the Mother, the Son and Daughter, and the Living Spirit of Esus. Faith is courage symbolized by the lion.

When the two gendered paths merge they pass through the narrow of the First Truth and stand together in the Light of deity. In deity there is no separation, and time does not exist and gender becomes whole in deity and all is in Harmony in the Garden of Idun (Eden).

56

What Are the Distinguishing Differences between the First and Second Paths?

The First Path is the circular path of the outer stone gates of timely clerical organization of words in statement of what 'we are' in each instant of knowing. All other words inherent in the preceding beginning time are in Secular notation that find their ending place in what is 'to be' upon the straightened paths of the completing wholeness of the holiday gates of the Maternal and Paternal Beings that enter deity and stand in the Light of all that is together in Lif in the ending time of Ragnarok.

To speak of words deeply ingrained in eternity is to speak of one's own eternal Being. All else is repetitive in circular meaning upon the First Path and proceeds into the Mneme upon the Second.

Upon the Second Path one passes through the narrow of the First Truth leading to deity to once more stand in the brilliant Light of the beginning time.

Samhain is the memorial day of all who have departed and in saintly Purpose passed through the narrow to enter upon the Second Path.

The celebration of Samhain begins on Allhallows Eve (Oct 31, Halloween) in purification. The following day is Allhallows Day, the day of the new Light (Nova) that begins on November 1st.

90

Solemnization upon the Second Path occurs between Samhain and Beltane—called the two fires of Bel. At Beltane, May 1st, May Day, all household fires are extinguished and rekindled in the evening announcing the end of the winter grazing season and the beginning of the planting season.

57

How Have the Stones Changed over the Years?

During the reign of the emperor Claudius, the Roman general Vespasian came to the great stone circle in A.D. 48 and pulled down the great stone called Truth and the lintel stone of Life fell upon it and was shattered. Only the stone of Love remained standing. The Children of Deis were driven outward, devoutly innocent to all worldly harmful intent, and were sent into exile on the island of Anglesey. During the reign of Nero, the Roman general Agricola brought the legions to the island in A.D. 61 and slew the remaining few.

That which possesses an infinite quality and that which is eternal are said to be Absolute.

Truth is infinite, and Love is eternal. The Love of Truth is Life, therefore, Life is the product of that which is infinite and eternal. Life is the only quality which is both infinite and eternal.

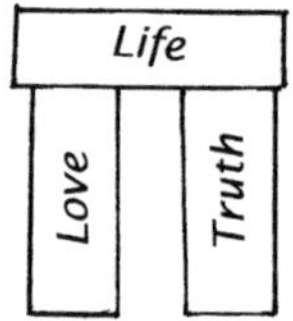

58

What Is Love?

There are two forms of love bestowed upon the bicameral nature of mankind.

In heaven Love is to be born as a deity (duality) within the instant wholeness of the Perfect Image in each word perceived as meaning upon the First Path.

Upon the Second Path in Idun's Garden of Creation Love is defined as being born in the Highest Expression of Freedom, which is the First Principle of the Ennead.

When there is both Perfection of Image and the Highest Expression of Freedom there is Unification in meaning and the unity of wholeness in Purpose and Life is complete.

59

How Does One Enter the Second Path from the Repetitive First Path of the Outer Circle of Stonehenge?

To enter the Second Path one must pass through the center trilith in the purity of perfect gendered form and stand in the Singular Light of Deity.

Passage through the center trilith begins with the Principles of four fixed thoughts forming the four surfaces of the tetrahedron which in conation proceeds to its final spherical configuration in wholeness without the need for further creation.

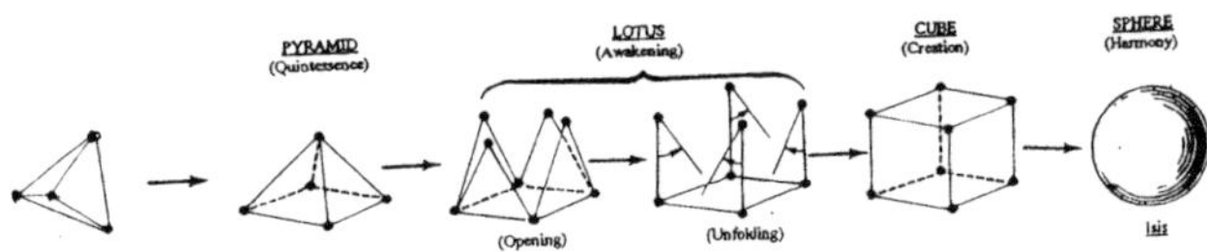

Summation proceeds to the limits → of necessity 'to be' within a second and final integration and then in perfect repetitive order to the instant of each particular case to find meaning within the descriptive text of each word. Each instant attained in this fashion becomes the power that comes into our Name, for there is only one instant and it is integrated within the fulcrum balance of the Name.

This is the fourth teaching of the Quadriga that is never written.

60

What Is the Title of the Fourth Teaching of the Quadriga and Why Is It Never Written?

The fourth teaching of the Quadriga is called the Right Hand of Deis. The fourth teaching is the teaching of the baptised Name. The Name is the gathering central fulcrum point of the instant of all words. There is only one attractive instant and it is present as the fulcrum point of the baptised Name.

The Name is the eye that cannot see itself, it is but a single reflection of wholeness (n-1).

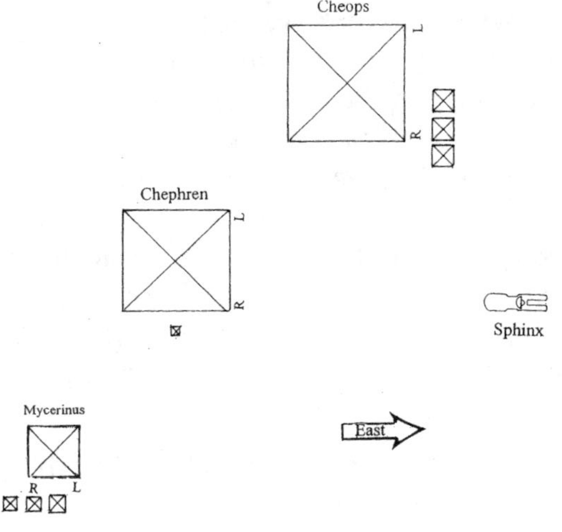

61

How Has the Celebration of the Sacraments Affected the Two Paths within the Inner Circle of Stonehenge?

In the same year in which he took Empirical office at Bizan A.D. 325 the emperor Constantine summoned the Council into holy session at Nicaea to establish a national common creed of belief.

The Nicene creed partly postulates the triunal elements of the God-head but completely eliminates the Matriarchal path of the Mother and Daughter within the Inner Circle in favor of the Patriarchal Path of the Father and Son and speaks only of Christos and not Esus, the intermediate Spiritual nature between God and mankind.

Each path having the essential qualities of a different nature. The heteroousian path of deity is removed and is supplanted by the singular homoousian path of masculine gender.

Heteroousian Path	Homoousian Path
Mother (Love)	Father (Truth)
Spirit (Virtue)	Spirit (Wisdom)
Daughter (Faith)	Son (Understanding)

Consubstantiation during Eucharist is the celebration of the Tarquinian cannibalistic feast of very ancient times and is designed in its modern interpretation to supplant the act of All-giving and All-receiving.

62

How Shall We Ask? How Shall We Give?

In wisdom Ask, and in Virtue give. Wisdom and Virtue are the inseparable qualities of the deity within the Living Spirit.

That which receives Life and is Alive are the inseparable qualities of Understanding and Faith in the Son and Daughter.

That which gives Life is Truth and Love and these are the qualities of the Father and the Mother.

The Preamble at the Prayer Stone

Conceived in Truth sustained by Love, infinite eternal Life our Father and Mother Above.

In Wisdom Ask, in Virtue Give, and in this Holy Spirit Live.

To Understand and keep Faith, the Son and the Daughter Alive in this our Grace.

The preamble is then followed by the Invocation.

63

What Is the Origin and Meaning of the Celebration of All-giving All-receiving?

In order to correct errors in the Roman calendar, Cleopatra suggested that Caesar extend the yearly celebration of the Saturnalia to include a fifth day called the Christos Mass in honor of their firstborn child, Caesarion. The occurrence of the five days of celebration of the Saturnalia were adjusted to correspond with the five hollow-days of the Celtic Yule-tide observance which now extend as holidays between Christmas and New Year's Day.

There is a saintly class, a priestly class, known jovially as the Santa Clause who maintain the corollary of beginning belief that it is better to give than to receive. Yet every gift is received of the omnipotent. And still they continue to observe the Yule Tide tree and its beginning meaning in the giving Spirit of Esus, the Carpenter Spirit that builds the chariot (carrier, car) that can enter all places, even through a household chimney. And even such, there are those who continue to observe the Kingly Spirit of Christos in receiving only as an heir apparent and in their merriment honor all and neglect the giving Spirit of Esus.

Such are the changes that have come about that the Hollow-day season is now a time of All-giving All-receiving and all is made whole again in happiness. Thus is eternal Faith and everlasting Hope born again of the provident and

hopeful Spirits of Esus and Christos in All-giving All-
receiving omnipotent Being and all is in all made whole
again in joyful song.